||||| ||| ||||| ||||| ||||| |||||
G000075122

Prayer

THE **MAN**UAL

BIBLE NOTES FOR MEN

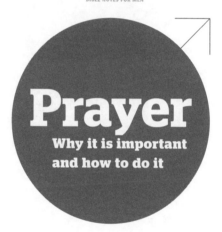

Prayer

**Why it is important
and how to do it**

NATHAN BLACKABY
WITH STEPHEN MCGUIRE

CWR

Copyright © Nathan Blackaby 2016

Published 2017 by CWR, Waverley Abbey House, Waverley Lane, Farnham,
Surrey GU9 8EP, UK. CWR is a Registered Charity – Number 294387 and a
Limited Company registered in England – Registration Number 1990308.

The right of Nathan Blackaby and Stephen McGuire to be identified as the
authors of this work has been asserted by them in accordance with the
Copyright, Designs and Patents Act 1988.

All rights reserved. No part of this publication may be reproduced, stored in
a retrieval system, or transmitted, in any form or by any means, electronic,
mechanical, photocopying, recording or otherwise, without the prior
permission in writing of CWR.

For a list of National Distributors visit www.cwr.org.uk/distributors

Unless otherwise indicated, all Scripture references are from the Holy Bible:
New Living Translation, copyright © 1996, 2004, 2015 by Tyndale House
Foundation. Used by permission of Tyndale House Publishers Inc., Carol Stream,
Illinois 60188. All rights reserved. Scripture marked ESV is taken from the ESV®
Bible (The Holy Bible, English Standard Version®). ESV® Permanent Text Edition®
(2016). Copyright © 2001 by Crossway, a publishing ministry of Good News
Publishers. All rights reserved.

Concept development, editing, design and production by CWR

Printed in the UK by Linney

ISBN: 978-1-78259-676-9

Nathan

Stephen

Nathan Blackaby is the Executive Director of CVM (Christian Vision for Men), a global movement focused on introducing men to Jesus Christ. Nathan leads the team at CVM, speaking to and reaching thousands of men each year with the gospel.

Formerly working as the Director of CVM in Scotland, Stephen McGuire is now a Pastor at Larbert Pentecostal Church and loves to see people fulfil their potential. He regularly embarrasses himself trying to lift weights in the gym and taking on silly swimming challenges.

Contents

Part 3: The Journey
Stephen McGuire

Introduction

What's praying all about? How do you pray? What should you be saying? Is there some kind of special way of praying or a secret formula? Jesus gave a prayer outline to His disciples (His closest friends), and you can check it out in the Bible (look for Matthew 6:9-13) if you're after a place to start.

Jesus also demonstrated prayer in loads of other ways – praying for the sick, praying for people in need of a miracle, praying for food, safety, guidance, wisdom, prayers of thanks and even crying out in prayer in really desperate times – and His disciples saw this and did the same thing.

This got me thinking; prayer is an incredible way in which you can be 100% real – just you and God. You don't need to get the words right, you don't need to put on a suit and carry a big leather Bible, you don't even need to say 'Amen'. Prayer is something you can discover, develop and build in your life; prayer can become natural and even something you love to do.

Let's be honest, sometimes you won't think to pray, and other times you will. Sometimes you will feel like your prayers are really landing, and at other times you won't feel that they are. I think that's normal. Our prayer life is something we build, train, strengthen and develop.

Maybe you already pray for hours on end – great! Maybe you have never prayed before and the whole idea seems a little bit odd – great! The point is that prayer is an amazing conversation with the living God that fuels, inspires, directs and motivates our faith and lives every day. This book is not a collection of prayers for you to copy; it is an invitation to be honest and start talking to God. You might find you set time aside first thing in the morning or at some other point in the day. Whenever you do it, do it.

In this book we'll explore how a king in the Bible called David discovered authentic prayer through the good times, the bad times and even the ugly times. Fears, doubts, questions, plans, hopes, dreams, frustrations, epic failures and glorious wins can be used as prayers, and I believe God wants to hear about this stuff because it's us and our lives – it's real and He loves that. Not all the psalms we will look at were written by David, but they express the stuff that matters, and fuel a life of prayer.

Let's get going.

PART 1

The Good

01 Hunger

'As the deer longs for streams of water, so I long for you, O God. I thirst for God, the living God.'

Psalm 42:1-2

Longing after God... what's that all about? Does this Bible verse sound a bit strange to you? Maybe a bit flowery or over the top? Well, you might be surprised to discover that the writer of this psalm, King David, was a serious, battle-scarred warrior who led a mighty and notorious band of men through some of the most violent and chilling missions recorded in the Bible. He was no stranger to war, and yet he also managed to express some of the most tender, dramatic, heartfelt prayers.

Compared to other poetry, there's something very different about the psalms – something powerful. They bite with an authenticity, and I think that's something most of us men want to apply to our own prayer lives. David's prayers aren't wishy-washy; they're gutsy.

This short verse makes a point that is vital for our prayer life and relationship with God: we need a hunger or a thirst for knowing God. And not just mild, 'take it or leave it' hunger, but a serious, life-depending kind of hunger. But what if we're not 'hungry or thirsty' for God? It's true, we can miss this because we try to fill the space with other things. Work, holidays, family, stuff – both good and bad. So we struggle to see the real need in our lives. But as we discover more about God, we see how His purposes and His presence in our lives is like food and water – it sustains us and gives us strength.

This verse shows us that David didn't hold back. He told God exactly what he thought. Can we really be that honest with God? Can we shout out to God when we see all the evil in the world, or our families and friends are struggling? Can we call out to God with the same intensity when life is sweet and we can see God doing stuff in and around our lives? Can we shout out the names of our family, asking God to reach them as He is reaching out to us?

YES! In prayer, bring your life, wins and fails to God. Just bring you.

Start to tell God about the stuff on your heart right now, and ask Him to help you develop a hunger for prayer and for Him.

02
Trust

'Even when I walk through the darkest valley, I will not be afraid, for you are close beside me.'

Psalm 23:4

Sometimes I don't realise how much trust I have until it is put to the test. Like a bungee rope – you trust it's the right one for you (and your extra 'winter weight' has been accounted for), but until you actually jump, your trust is only theoretical.

I invited a mate once to jump on the back of my Honda CBR600 when I went for a ride. He did, and I think it was the first time he'd ever prayed! He had to trust me – he was all in – but boy, did he get off that bike in a bad way (and I didn't even go that fast!)...

In this psalm, David is saying that even when he walks in the darkest valleys, he will choose not to fear. And this is something he actually lived out – David had been down those dark valleys that we sometimes journey along. This is not some abstract trust here – this just got real!

I remember walking into an overcrowded Brazilian prison where I was part of a team speaking to the guys and praying together. As we walked in I was praying silently, but as the door actually closed behind me, and I realised I was shut inside a prison built for 100 men with over a thousand in it, my prayers got real. With just my Bible under my arm, my trust was being put to the test. It was the most alive I had felt for a long time. I was on the edge, where my praying met with the experience, the moment and the reality.

David is speaking out trust here, directly into the situations he is facing, despite his feelings. I like that, and don't do it enough. This is a great way to pray – thanking God by speaking out and declaring that He is trustworthy.

You might be about to enter 'the valley', or even be in the valley of trouble right now, but that's where trust starts to really matter. Speak it out, thank God for who He is, and know that He is the one who guides us as we trust Him.

Take some time today to speak out to God the ways in which you trust Him or need to trust Him – that's prayer! For your family, your mates, work and health.

---

03 Faithfulness

'The LORD will work out his plans for my life—for your faithful love, O LORD, endures forever.' `Psalm 138:8`

I remember my dad telling me once: 'You only need a small seed of faith in God because He is completely faithful.' I like that. You see, I don't think God is asking us to try to understand all His ways and why things are happening or not happening. We won't be able to figure that out anyway! He simply calls us to let Him into our lives.

In 2014 I moved my family to Derbyshire to take on a role within CVM. With our three young children, and my wife wrestling with a disability, we started to struggle. In desperation, I knew God had spoken to me. It wasn't an audible voice, but through prayer and reading the Bible I had this deep conviction. But still, the reality was that the pressure we found ourselves under was crippling. Children, a new job, an ill wife, making new friends with little family around was a strain. Maybe you've been there.

Exhausted and low, I started to call out God's faithfulness, like David. My prayer was real and I began to just thank God for His plans, even the ones I couldn't see, all based on *His* faithfulness. Sure, I had my moments of doubt. I questioned if I had heard right, questioned the plan and why it felt like God had let His side of it go. But my prayers and needs were answered in the most amazing ways, and help arrived. My parents now live opposite us – literally in front of us – something I never saw coming. (No, I know what you're thinking; but it was a *good* answer to prayer for us!)

Looking back, I wrestled when I should have rested; I planned when I should have prayed. What about you? Know that God is faithful. He has a plan and while it might not be your plan, He has the bigger picture.

Spend some time reflecting on Jesus, and ask that you will know Him more in your own life. Talk to Him about your faith – where it is, what it looks like and what it needs.

04

Strength

'Let all that I am wait quietly before God, for my hope is in him.'

Psalm 62:5

King David was a man who knew battle. He looked out and saw vast armies of enemies pressing in on all sides... he definitely knew what pressure felt like. He witnessed personal victory and triumph, defeat, and even being a man on the run, seeking refuge. David was a king who fought and battled – he led men into combat, and men followed him, risking their lives serving at his side. Warrior strength was part of David's DNA.

On one occasion, King Saul, a man blinded by jealousy and hatred, was chasing David to kill him. Backed into a cave, David had a chance to kill Saul as he entered the cave too... but did he do it? Well, his mates encouraged him to, but no, David didn't do it. Instead, he showed amazing strength, but it came through brokenness and was like a moment of praise and rejoicing to God.

David came out of the cave behind Saul and lay on the floor. Bowing low, he surrendered. David spoke out to God in front of Saul and all his men, and he yielded his life and heart not to Saul but to God! Quietly, David bowed low in surrender to the God he worshipped and followed – a move that could have cost him his life! He could have run Saul through with his blade, letting out a victory shout as he did it, taking matters into his own hands and using his strength to 'fix' it. But he didn't; he showed strength in surrendering to God.

This is a real prayer of praise and hope in God. David was not trusting in his own strength but God's. It's a counter-cultural view of strength, but when we have total dependency on God, we're in the sweet spot.

What are you facing right now that has you fighting and wrestling in your own strength? Talk to God about it. How can He fight this battle for you?

04

05 Stillness

'Be still, and know that I am God!'
Psalm 46:10

Being 'still' is something that is difficult to do.
When I go away on holiday, my wife says that it
takes me a few days to 'switch off'. I've become
very used to noise and activity around me;
smartphones and tablets; rushing between
meetings; running the kids to their clubs. Stillness
is a rare thing. But why? What's the point? You
can't change the world by being still, right?

Prayer and stillness are keys to really seeing
and experiencing who God is, and finding out who
we are! If I see a problem or difficulty, I try to fix it. I
work hard to find ways to create, repair or improve.
I tried to do this for a long time as a Christian,
too – trying to read the right books, pray the right
prayers and better my relationship with God. But
here's the rub with this one, fellas: sometimes we
need to just be still, and let God show us who He is.

A bloke in the Bible called Elijah was invited
by God to stand still and glimpse the presence of
God. This guy was a prophet, which means God
would speak to him and give him a message for
the people who were following God. (Sometimes

these messages and the ways they were delivered were brutal, to say the least!) Anyway, on one occasion after a proper battle, Elijah stood there on the mountainside and a windstorm smashed past. Nothing. Then an earthquake, followed by fire. Nothing. Then a whisper, moving past Elijah. Immediately, Elijah wrapped his face in his top and sensed the very presence of God in the stillness of that moment – in the whisper.

I think we need a bit of that – to be hit by the presence of God. Sure, it might be a windstorm that does it, but it might also be that whisper that needs you to be still and wait. The point is, when you hear and sense the presence of God, it's a game-changer. It was for Elijah, and it is for you and me.

Go for a walk alone. Each time your brain jumps in with ideas about different things, try to silence it and focus on Jesus. In the stillness, talk to Him about what's going on in your life. What is He saying back to you?

06

Triumph

'In your strength I can crush an army; with my God I can scale any wall.' **Psalm 18:29**

David doesn't use words here like, 'You make me feel dizzy when You are near.' Instead he praises God by saying things like, 'God, You are my fortress and power', and then throws in some gold like today's verse.

You might think that to be a Christian means walking about with a smile and using words like 'peace', 'gentleness' and 'care'. I want to praise my King in a different way. At times I have felt stifled, like I am supressing stuff that I can use to celebrate who God is to me and who He has made me to be!

It is good to be honest about what we like doing and how it makes us feel to celebrate our God-given strength and 'manliness'. But let's also communicate some of this side of us in prayer. Stuff like, 'God, You are like a consuming fire. You are incredible. Your power can crush my enemies and help me do the impossible. You have made me like this. I want to thank You. Teach me about my strength and my passion.'

In this psalm, David is praising God, and at the same time I think he is saying to God, 'When You are with me I can really be me. I can crush any enemies and I can climb any wall in my way.'

You might read that and wince at the war analogy. And that's OK – wince away, because it happened. But what I think is important here is that we smash small ideas and kick out hints of mediocrity. God invites us to celebrate that He can do all things; His strength is all we need and when we have it we can be part of the impossible. The stuff that fires us up can actually be helpful in how we express our heart to God.

What do you want to triumph over?

_____

Thank God for the victories and triumphs in your life. Invite Him to break stuff in you that needs to be dealt with, and build new stuff in its place. Now go and do the things God has given you a passion for!

_____

07

Justice

> 'Put your hope in the LORD.
> Travel steadily along his path.'
> **Psalm 37:34**

I remember watching *Judge Dredd* and loving the bit when a judge had to take 'the long walk'. If you don't know the film, the retiring judge, unwilling to take a desk job, would leave the corps through a ceremonial gun salute, take the 'Book of Law' and leave the city to face the lawless in the wastelands of earth, bringing them order and judgment. I loved it! Sylvester Stallone, as you might expect, smashed and punched his justice all over the place.

So what? Where is my deep spiritual devotional for today? Can I really punch people and show them I love Jesus?

When I read or watch the news, I often find myself weighed down by the injustice of it all. The corruption, lies and extortion. The exploitation. The gossip. Crime, trafficking, abuse and murder can leave us feeling like justice has been lost and our faith, if we are honest, can start to take a battering with all this stuff flying around.

This feeling of injustice is not new, and it got the heart of David too. And guess what, David turned it into praise (Psalm 37) and we can pray it as well.

God keeps His promises, and David knew it! Even though he couldn't understand the mess when he looked at the world, he knew God would act and make it right. Justice *will* be done one day. We simply need to trust that Jesus will bring His justice to an unjust world. Don't forget this side of God: He is judge, and one day will bring all things to account.

What's my part and yours in this? Go back to verse 34 and take another look at what David is suggesting. Put your hope in the *Lord* and travel steadily on *His* path! (Best not go around punching everyone with your 'fist of justice' like Judge Dredd, though...)

Let God know your frustrations and anger about the injustice you see. Ask Him to help you keep your feet on His path, and your trust in Him alone.

08

Bravery

'Wait patiently for the LORD.
Be brave and courageous.
Yes, wait patiently for the LORD.'
Psalm 27:14

What comes to mind when you think about bravery and courage? Maybe you think of daring acts of valour, fearlessness, audaciousness and boldness? I do, too, and the Bible is full of men who would not allow themselves to be mastered by fear or limited by doubt; men who took giant steps of faith against all reason and logic, and became part of a story they could never have imagined possible. Does that stir something in you? It does me. I want to be part of that; to know that adventure and risk.

I remember being really afraid once. It was on that church trip to Brazil I mentioned earlier... I honestly thought I would be killed in the rainforests in the process! I wanted to be a man who knew the path of bravery and courage in my walk with God, but this fear of being killed undid me. After some time I realised that I get to choose to live beyond these fears, but also that I had naively hoped that 'bravery' was something I could order online, go to checkout and select 'next day delivery', all while sitting on the couch in my pants.

What do bravery and courage look like for you, and how could you turn this into prayer? Maybe just starting to pray and thinking about this God stuff is pushing the limit anyway! Or maybe you have just become a Christian and you need that courage in the office, factory, garage, shop, school or home?

I love that scene in *Indiana Jones and the Last Crusade* where he has the faith to step out into the abyss and onto an invisible bridge. Our prayer lives can be a bit like that. But it's in prayer that we can find strength, *real* strength – not like the dude in the gym with arms the size of tree trunks, but a strength to face overwhelming odds and terrifying situations.

Do you need more bravery for telling people about your faith in Jesus? Or do you need God to put you in some places that will shake the dust off you a bit, so that you can rediscover what bravery really looks like as a Christian? Talk it out with God now. Be brave!

09

Get real

'My sins pile up so high I can't see my way out.' **Psalm 40:12**

Do you have an old friend, maybe from school or a previous job, who you just go straight into 'real' mode with, even if you haven't seen them for ages? No messing about, just honest and genuine. You might reminisce for ages and laugh, then get to the things that matters and talk about 'real stuff': the wins, fails, battles and disappointments.

David's faith in God and relationship with Him became so real that his communication with God reached this level of depth. Psalm 40 covers a lot of this, and is great for helping us pray. Take a look.

David celebrates that God has met with him, encouraged him and strengthened him. Then David talks to God about how he has been able to be open in his relationship with Him, not hiding his faith away. David talks about his troubles, problems and the sin that has piled high in his life to the point of stealing his courage. He asks God to rescue him again, to help him and bring justice to his enemies.

I've found that if I go through a time of not praying and just get busy doing my own thing, it can be really hard to start praying again. But it doesn't need to be! Think about it like those mates from school who you haven't seen in ages and finally meet up with again. You don't spend the whole night apologising or analysing all the reasons why you haven't talked for so long – you just talk! Start talking to God again. Laugh with Him. Be honest and real.

Being real with God as we pray is an act of worship. It shows that you trust Him with the most private affairs of your spirit. If you haven't prayed for a while, tell Him, and then get on with it. If life is tough, talk to God about it: talk about why it is tough and how it got that way. If things are going well you can bring that stuff to Him too.

Get real with God today. Plans, hopes, failures, trust, unbelief, worry or pain… tell Him as the friend who always invites you to be real. Let nothing about you be 'off limits' to God.

10
Shouting

'With my whole being, body and soul, I will shout joyfully to the living God.' Psalm 84:2

So, you might be reading this on the train (where I'm writing it) or in the early hours of the morning, so maybe wait until an appropriate time to give it a go – but shouting to God can be a prayer of praise too!

One year at The Gathering (CVM's annual men's festival), we had a cool guy called Dave Hearne from Global Adventure get a load of us shouting around the fire pit on the Saturday night. As a load of men called out to God in prayer, shouting out the names of family they wanted to bring before God, it was amazing – the guys loved it. Our voices are significant – we know that from just our own circles of influence and the impact we can have by using them, both positive and negative. But shouting out to God in prayer is a bit out there, right?

I'm not trying to raise an army of voice activists here, but I was silent for so long that I needed to shout a bit to get me moving again in prayer. I was too worried about fitting in, and not standing out or drawing attention to myself. We can quickly get into a pattern of talking to God that is meek and mild-mannered, quiet and still, and any drips of emotion and passion, anger, joy, frustration or energy can be lost. But we need that stuff!

Look at the psalm again: 'With my whole being, body and soul, I will shout joyfully to the living God.' Have you prayed like that recently? Really using your voice to call out to God? Try it! Go somewhere and shout out – really use your voice to shout the names of those you love, giving them to God. Shout out fears and failings if you want. (Obviously check who is around!) I remember once being at a men's weekend where we wrote out our sins and fears on a piece of paper, wrapped them around a stone and threw them into the sea. As I threw mine, the wind unwrapped it and my sin-filled paper flew back to me, open for all to read, while the stone went out to sea! It's funny now, but it wasn't at the time...

Call out the stuff that matters to you and pray, while shouting! And while you're at it, why not speak out for somebody else?

10

PART 2

The Bad

11
Rally points

'But you have raised a banner for those who fear you—a rallying point in the face of attack.' **Psalm 60:4**

In the psalms we see a real honesty and willingness to talk to God about the good things in life when it's all going swimmingly, but also about the bad stuff. When life was peachy, David thanked God and celebrated who He is, but even when life was bad and trouble or enemies were at the door, David talked to God and celebrated who He is during those times too!

David often wrote psalms reflecting on something that had happened; war, conflict, trouble, an enemy or even a personal failure or mistake. There was a lot going on in his life and he took it all to God: frustrations, cares, anxiety, brokenness and weakness.

This psalm was written off the back of war. David starts by calling out to God in the face of disaster and destruction. Made desperate by what was going on, he felt rejected, broken and shaken, and he tells God all about it.

Then, in the middle - as is so common in the psalms - is a moment of relief and rescue, like a rally point and a place of shelter to regroup and take stock in the heat of the attack.

You might be asking, 'What is that place? How can I find one of those, and what happens there?' The answer is God Himself, and I believe that our prayer life and discipline will help us to discover this even more. Being in His presence is where we are safe; where we are patched up for the next round of combat.

David trusted. He called out the troubles, reaffirmed his trust and waited on the Lord for help and power for each day. Rally points in the face of our enemy are moments when you meet with God and glimpse again who He is and what He does. All powerful, all mighty, Prince of peace and King of kings.

Talk to God, your rally point, in the middle of trouble. Tell Him honestly about it. Cry out, call out or whisper – just tell Him and be renewed in the fight.

12

Brokenness

> 'The sacrifice you desire is a broken spirit. You will not reject a broken and repentant heart, O God.'
> **Psalm 51:17**

This time, David is broken. He has committed adultery and tried to cover it all up by getting an innocent man killed. The Bible tells us that a prophet visits David and brings truth from God, revealing David's sin and failed cover-up job (my mate Stephen will talk about that later on in this book).

With so much to be explored in this psalm, the best place to start is by reading it over a couple of times. Do that now. Seriously. This little book will be waiting right here.

Back yet? What did you discover? Go and read it again... slower this time! When I did this I realised something: being broken with God is a good thing.

If I come to your house and throw a brick through your window, two things will happen. First, I will probably get removed from your Christmas card list; and second, you will have a window that is no longer fit for purpose. It will be smashed and broken and your delicate lace curtains will be in tatters.

In the world around us, stuff breaking is usually a bad thing, but it is different with God when *we* are broken. David discovered that through this really difficult period in his life, his prayer was not about what he could offer God, or say or do or sacrifice. The heart of the matter was a matter of the heart. (Like what I did there?)

When we let God break stuff in our lives, deep in us, it doesn't ruin us and render us useless; it sharpens, awakens and mobilises the Spirit within. David threw all this out to God in prayer – all of it – and came to a place of brokenness as God dealt with him, tearing down the old and building up the new. This is really empowering, and we mustn't skip it just because it hurts!

Ask God if there are things in your life that need to be broken. Invite God in as you dig deep and talk to Him. The Holy Spirit will shine a light on the bits that need breaking. As He does, don't resist. Surrender them and you will be rebuilt stronger than before!

---

13 Storms

'Give your burdens to the LORD, and he will take care of you.' Psalm 55:22

Recently, my wife and I went walking in the Peak District. Time is valuable for us as a couple – a rare treat! I had a morning off work so we put on our boots and ventured outside. It was a cold and wet day, but we wanted to walk as the children were all at school.

As we got to this higher point on the walk, the wind and the rain really picked up. It was like a windstorm pushing us around, with horizontal rain soaking us completely (very romantic...). We looked around for shelter and found a natural hollow in the ground, about the size of the average living room. We went and sat down in this massive dip, which had clearly had about a thousand sheep and cows using it as a toilet. Out of the wind and the rain we just sat in silence, resting as the storm raged around us.

Storms happen in our lives, and as Christian men we are not excluded from this reality. They can happen for all sorts of reasons and at all sorts of inconvenient times. The question is, what do we do?

David turned it into a reason to talk to God. Take a look at Psalm 55 and you will soon see the type of storm and situation David was in. Fear and terror were gripping him, and he wanted to fly away and leave it all behind. David makes his case before God and tells Him what's going on.

David's relationship with God saw him through storms, family disasters and several enemies, and he kept on finding these shelters in Him. David called out that God would rescue, God would hear his voice, and God would be his victory. This was often before David had even seen any evidence of a victory!

I don't know the storm you might be in, or the one that you haven't even seen yet, but know that you can pray and find that shelter – that place with God that won't mean the storm always passes you, but in it you will know peace as David did.

Tell God about the storm you're in, and ask Him to show you His plan and purpose. Ask Him to give you strength.

13

14 Remember

> 'Remember me, LORD, when you show favor to your people; come near and rescue me.' **Psalm 106:4**

When I was still in school, a good mate of mine let it slip that he fancied a particular girl. He wouldn't tell anyone who it was for fear of it getting out and potentially causing himself embarrassment. Well, being the good mate that I was back then, I set about convincing him that my word was like an unbreakable bond, a promise and a covenant between him and me. If he told me her name it would never be uttered again and I would take his secret to my grave.

He told me her name, so I immediately announced it to the school.

We look back now and laugh, but he definitely wasn't laughing at the time. I felt pretty terrible about not keeping my promise.

The amazing thing about God is that He remembers His promises; no wavering, no mistakes. It's just who He is. The early group of people who God began revealing His plans to were the Israelites. As a people, they'd been enslaved in Egypt, and God rescued them.

The Israelites made promises to God all the time and then forgot about them, but God never forgot His promises to them. He kept His side of the deal and still does with you and me. When the psalmist says, 'Remember me, LORD', he's saying that he wants in on that. We might feel like God has forgotten us sometimes, but He hasn't.

But there is something God deliberately doesn't remember. When we mess up, and then go to Him to say we're sorry and sort things out, He dropkicks that sin out of the park. God doesn't wink at the mess in our lives and give us a knowing nod of the head. Instead, He remembers the life that paid the price: His Son. Jesus took our sin on the cross, so when God promises you forgiveness He means it. *Your* sin. He actually chooses to *not* remember it because of what Jesus did – it was taken from you and put on Him!

It's worth remembering that.

God will never, ever forget about you. How could you remember Him more throughout your day?

14

15

Frustrations

'O God, why have you rejected us so long? Why is your anger so intense against the sheep of your own pasture?' **Psalm 74:1**

Have you ever shouted a prayer out to God in frustration? Anger? Disappointment? Despair? I have, and as far as I can see in the Bible, it's allowed. My wife struggles with a disability, and there has been no shortage of frustration prayers coming from our household. 'God, why don't you answer me? Why won't you heal her? Why has this gone on for so long? When will you do something? Why have you left us?' Well, take courage – this is not new, and has been on the hearts of many people who have turned to God in prayer.

This psalm talks about destruction. All around them, the people of God had seen destruction, and in particular the destruction of their temple; their precious place of worship. But what seemed to hurt them the most was their sense of abandonment. 'Where are you, God, and why is this happening? Am I being punished? Where's the breakthrough I need so badly?'

Does that sound like you today? Well... put your boots on and go for a walk outside.

This may seem like strange advice, but let me explain. In this psalm, even though the people were having a proper shout at God for all the rubbish they were going through, they still saw that God loved them. How? How is it possible for them or for me or you at this moment?

The answer is that they saw God's love just by looking at creation (have a look at Psalm 74:12-17). They looked around, and even in the middle of chaos and disaster, they saw evidence of the creator God everywhere; they saw His power and presence, and it encouraged them.

Get outside on your own. Get yourself into the wilderness, a bit of space, and meet with Him. Many of my darkest hours have seen light once I immerse myself in God's creation. He has met me through it.

If you're feeling frustrated, try using this prayer as a starting point: 'God, would You show me You're still there. In this mess and chaos, still my heart and mind so I can see straight. My hurt and my frustration are real. I give them to You. Help me. Amen.'

---

16 Rescue

'But you are always the same;
you will live forever.' **Psalm 102:27**

Have you ever been totally overwhelmed? Do you feel overwhelmed right now? If you have or are, then stop what you're doing, talk to God and read this psalm, because it is written from a place where life's struggles and trials seem impossible to conquer. The psalmist needs a-rescuing.

I remember being unemployed for a while. And not only that, I was living in a borrowed house and only had a month left in it. I had just come back from honeymooning with my beautiful new wife, but my plan to provide for her, be her man and not see her struggle was about as solid as a house of cards. With no money, the reality of potential homelessness just a month away and no job or way out, I was overwhelmed. It felt like a dark cloud that I could almost reach out and grab.

This might seem like a strange story to use when talking about prayer. Prayer is for church on a Sunday, or saying grace at dinner, right?

Not this time. Prayer was all I had and I really did need a rescue.

This psalm calls out to God in prayer from a seemingly hopeless place, yet it discovers hope not in what the eyes can see, but what the heart chooses to remember. We are part of a bigger picture. God who was, and is, and is to come, is not limited by time or circumstances. Our hope is in something that time, rust or thieves can never destroy.

At that time, all I could do was sing out to God in prayer (actually, 'squawk' might be a better word!), thanking Him that He will be forever. My time will come and go, my struggles will come and go, but I can always cry out to God to rescue me.

He did. He lifts me back to my feet – again, and again, and again.

Try singing out Exodus 15:2, or put it in your own words: 'The Lord is my strength and my song, and he has become my salvation; this is my God, and I will praise Him' (ESV).

17
Waiting

'Listen to my voice in the morning, LORD. Each morning I bring my requests to you and wait expectantly.' **Psalm 5:3**

Sometimes our biggest challenge can come in the form of trying to work out what's next in life. Jobs, home, family, school, college, university, where, how, what, when... Does any of that resonate with you?

We can lie awake at night churning this stuff around in our heads and hearts, losing sleep and losing patience. Guess what the answer is? Pray!

Praying about your future doesn't mean you'll get a finger from heaven pointing at an atlas with specific coordinates (though that *could* happen...). What you will discover is the presence of God in your life in a new way, because that's what God does. He wants to meet you, guide you and sharpen your life.

In Psalm 5, David is seeking God for direction. 'Which way, God? There are traps and potential pitfalls and wrong turns all around me. Which way?' This is a prayer that is asking God to guide and speak directly into his situation.

There have been plenty of times when I've found myself feeling totally lost and struggling to navigate things on my own. At times like these, it really is as simple as looking 'up'.

Let me explain. For me, looking 'up' took some effort. I had to actively carve out time early in the morning before my kids woke up to seek God and wait on Him. (It doesn't need to be the morning, of course. That's just what worked best for me, but it could be a different time for you.) But creating this rhythm in my life did more than I can tell you. It directed some of the biggest decisions I have made to date. I walked, I listened, I read, and I prayed.

The prayer is simple, based on Psalm 5:8: 'Make Your way straight before my face, Lord.'

Set aside some time to read or listen to the Bible and talk to God. Start to intentionally 'look up' each day in prayer, asking God to speak into your situation and give you some direction. See how this rhythm changes your life!

18
Fear

> 'God is an honest judge. He is angry with the wicked every day. If a person does not repent, God will sharpen his sword; he will bend and string his bow.' **Psalm 7:11-12**

This might seem like a strange way of countering fear in our lives, but I want to try it. We often hear a side of God presented that is the shepherd who loves the sheep in His care, and of course this is amazing and powerful. You can find loads of verses in the Bible where God tells us really clearly to not be afraid, and to not let fear dominate our hearts and minds. But what is often missed out is that God is also described in the Bible as a divine warrior, who bends His bow and sharpens His sword for holy and divine judgment, and in some way this helps our fear. Hmm... that's a bit different, isn't it? This is a bit like you saying to fear, 'My dad is bigger than your dad!'

What does this have to do with the fear you might be feeling about something in your life right now? Well, when writing this psalm, David was in a place of fear – people wanted to kill him and destroy him - and he found peace in this way of thinking about God as a just judge and warrior.

Proverbs 9:10 talks about the fear of the Lord being the beginning of wisdom! This isn't the same as hiding from a parent in fear when you have smashed a window playing football. This is a deeper meaning of fear that looks more like reverence. It's a fear that doesn't create the desire to escape; it calls for the opposite. It calls us to come close in awe and wonder, in respect and submission, to the power and majesty of God, because He judges, He has the final say and all authority is His.

Does that encourage you? The psalmist found that when he talked to God like that it steadied his heart and his mind, and even turned his fears into worship, praising God!

Ask God to help you see Him as warrior and judge, and that He will teach you a fear and astonishment in Him that will sustain and comfort you in your time of fear.

18

19

Innocence

'I wash my hands to declare my innocence. I come to your altar, O LORD, singing a song of thanksgiving and telling of all your wonders.' **Psalm 26:6-7**

During the psalm-writing period of biblical history, there was a set routine for the sacrifice of animals so that a man, woman or community could be 'made clean' (have their sins removed) in order to be fit to worship God. When Jesus died on the cross, this system was scrapped. He became the ultimate sacrifice that paid for all of humanity's sin, ever. His blood made us clean. And at the moment Jesus died, the huge curtain in the temple, which kept ordinary, sinful people out of the 'holy of holies', was ripped from top (heaven) to bottom (earth).

Why is this important? It is important for us as men, and for all people generally, to know that when Jesus died for us, He forgave our sins. He made us right with God, and He declared us innocent once and for all time.

This matters – this prayer *really* matters. You might struggle with the past; maybe you have lost that innocence in the wrong choices you have made. Maybe porn has robbed it from you, or things you've said or done that have torn apart people around you. The thought of your innocence might seem like a lifetime ago, far beyond reach, but it's not. If you want to tell people how good God has been, you can, because Jesus has declared you INNOCENT! He has wiped the slate clean. The past has been dealt with. You are a new man!

However you lost your sense of innocence, you need to know it has been returned. I need to know it too! Thank You, Jesus.

It was costly for Jesus to buy back your innocence. Thank Him today, and ask Him to show you what it really means.

---

20 Down but not out

'I pray to you, O LORD, my rock. Do not turn a deaf ear to me. For if you are silent, I might as well give up and die.' **Psalm 28:1**

Here's another amazing psalm from David, the mighty man of God. In this one you can see him go from crisis in life to confidence in God. At CVM we have a saying about being knocked down but never knocked out – we call this 'resurrection DNA'. We keep getting up because of Jesus' life empowering us. Here in this psalm and prayer there is even more for us to see.

A mate of mine a while ago showed me a journal of his where he writes His prayers out, like letters to God. He sometimes even writes 'Dear Dad' and finishes them 'From James, Your son'. At first I wasn't sure about it, but I gave it a go.

I started to write my own letters. Some were 'Thank You' letters, and some were more along the lines of, 'What on earth is going on?' Lots of them were about the hits and knocks I was taking in life and how that made me feel, and I needed to get it all down on the page. The thing is, as I continue to write more (as I still do), I sometimes look back at the old 'letters', and when I see what I have written in the past I realise something: I was down then but not out, never out.

David, when he writes this psalm, is down but not out. He hits the bottom of the pit but then discovers he can get back out again. Sometimes we need to use this in the way we pray, almost like looking back and forward at the same time. You might be down and feeling seriously out today. If guilt and shame are holding you down there, hand them over to God. Get up and say, 'God, here I am.'

If you're in that place of down and out, spend some time calling out to God in prayer. And if you're in a good place right now, why not spend some time praying for someone you know who may need God right now? Ask for His hand to pull them back up again.

PART 3

The Journey

Stephen McGuire

21 Honesty

'Against you, and you alone, have I sinned; I have done what is evil in your sight.' **Psalm 51:4**

Honesty is a character trait that we would all love to say we have in abundance. But in reality, if we are genuinely honest with ourselves, we often slip up and fail. (I mean, who is going to know about that little lie…?) Honestly, we're not always honest.

Nathan looked at this psalm on Day 12, and how God uses our brokenness – but I want to take another look at it. In this psalm, David is humbling himself by being open and honest with God about his ill-advised and frankly disastrous affair with Bathsheba.

David had gone to extraordinary lengths to conceal his affair, even to the point of arranging for Bathsheba's husband, who had pledged his allegiance to David, to be killed. David thought he had covered all his tracks. Surely no one would know what he had got up to. But God knew, just as He knows all our slip-ups and failures.

I love that after the prophet Nathan's confrontation, the first place David went was to God in prayer. He was incredibly honest in admitting his failings, asking for forgiveness and for God's help to change and stop repeating the same mistakes over and over. And I don't think this was him falling on his sword, either. This was genuine repentence. His secret was out, and what a relief.

We all make mistakes. The truth can be hard, but it does set us free. Too often I've met people who've ended up in worse situations than they would have been in if they hadn't tried to cover their tracks in the first place.

It's a great model for us to follow, that in our prayer life we can confess the mess to God and trust and know that we *will* be forgiven (1 John 1:9).

Take some time today to tell God the ways in which you have slipped up, no matter how big or small. Be honest with yourself and with God.

---

22 Despair

> 'From the depths of despair,
> O LORD, I call for your help.'
> **Psalm 130:1**

The chances are, we will all face (or have faced) deep despair. It might be bereavement, a sudden job loss, bad health or some other reason, big or small, that drags us down into the depths of despair. Often we don't know which direction to turn in, who to talk to or who to seek help from. Prayer is often at the bottom of our list of actions.

I know this only too well. A few years back I was going through a really tough time – things at home, work and, yes, even church were tough. Life was hard and I was quickly heading south on a downward spiral. I was looking everywhere for help, except in the place that ought to have been top of my list. Praying wasn't even on my radar; it didn't compute in my thinking. How wrong I was.

While we don't know the exact details of the situation that the writer of Psalm 130 is in, we can very much imagine him being in a place where he is in desperate need of the mercy of God, whether it is circumstances of great suffering, just living in a messed up world, or if he had messed up yet again. However, the writer is so sure that God would reach down into the depths of his despair. By the end of the psalm he is praising God and encouraging all of Israel to put their whole hope in Him.

So what about us? Where do we turn to when we feel we've hit rock-bottom? Can we make prayer our first port of call? Can we trust that God will reach down into our pit and pull us up? When I was in my own season of despair, it was only when I prayed that things began to turn around and I could see light at the end of the tunnel. The lesson for me: prayer comes first!

Take some time today to speak out to God about the struggles you have – both big and small – and trust that He will hear and answer those prayers.

23

Repent and be restored

'But I would feed you with the finest wheat. I would satisfy you with wild honey from the rock.'
Psalm 81:16

If we read through Psalm 81 we see the writer pondering over the history of Israel, and what might have been. Let's recap – Israel was the group of people who God started to reveal His rescue mission to in the Old Testament. The psalmist imagines God lamenting their wasted potential, considering what He could have done for them and through them, if only they had obeyed Him.

How often do we reflect on our lives, thinking about what might have been. 'If only I hadn't made that bad choice; if only I hadn't made those comments that pulled that person down. If only...'

We can waste countless hours doing an autopsy on the past, but there's nothing we can do to change it. And we don't enjoy feeling like we've wasted parts of our lives! Much like the people of Israel, when we ignore God's calling and guidance and follow our own devices (Psalm 81: 12), we can end up with those 'what might have been' moments.

I have discovered that the way to avoid a wasted life is to live in obedience to God, even though this is no walk in the park! I often mess up, ignore God's way and go my own way. But when that happens I have a choice. I can either just carry on and end up regretting the past, or I can turn to God in prayer, repenting (literally turning away from what we have done wrong, and turning back to God), asking for His forgiveness and then being restored back into right relationship with Him.

God is in the business of restoring lives. When a person trusts in Jesus Christ as Saviour, there is new hope. And it all starts with a simple prayer: 'Lord, I'm sorry.'

Take some time today to speak out to God about the 'what might have been' moments in your life. What are your regrets? Ask Him to use the time you feel that you might have wasted.

24

Integrity

'I can never get away from your presence!' **Psalm 139:7**

This has to be one of my favourite psalms. It really challenges me, and I think it shows us a lot of the different aspects of God's character. The one aspect that challenges me the most is His omniscience – the fact that He knows *everything*.

The psalm tells us that God knows our habits, good and bad (v3). He knows every word we say (v4), and in verse 2 He knows our every thought... scary stuff! Psalm 139:6, loosely translated, says, 'That blows me away!' David is essentially saying, 'Such knowledge is too bonkers for me to grasp; too massive for my brain.' I feel the same way!

How can you fathom a God who knows every thought that you've ever had, the same being true for all those other billions of people on the planet? It just blows my mind! But the challenge I take from this applies to our integrity. Do we always say and do the same in private, when no one is looking, as we say and do in public?

Often I feel determined to live out my life with total integrity – and this might last for a few days, or even a week, if I'm on a roll. But then real life starts kicking in. The pressures of work start weighing on my mind. The kids start playing up, driving me towards breaking point. The bills are coming in while my bank balance is nervously dwindling.

Real life creeps up on us, and soon we start forgetting the God stuff. We struggle to stay on 'the narrow road' as the Bible calls it, and our integrity can be compromised. The real danger is when we think that no one is watching and that we can get away with things.

This psalm is clear that God sees and knows everything. We can't hide it from Him, but this is actually really freeing. In prayer we can stay plugged in to what God wants for our lives. Our integrity in the moments of pressure, crisis and heat will be built when we have a strong prayer life.

Ask God to reveal areas in your life where your integrity has slipped. Ask Him for forgiveness and for His help to be a real man of integrity.

---

25 Safety

'Keep me safe, O God, for I have come to you for refuge.' **Psalm 16:1**

Even if we live in a country that experiences relative safety compared to other parts of the world, we still do things every day to help safeguard our temporal (earthly) safety.

We instinctively try to protect ourselves and those we love and care for from harm and danger. We avoid risks that could kill us. We wear seatbelts in a car, and we wear cycle helmets on a bike. We try to exercise, eat healthily, and avoid smoking and junk foods that can potentially cause disease. We have smoke alarms, burglar alarms, bike locks and padlocks on the shed or garage. We lock the front door behind us when we leave the house and we look both ways before we cross a road.

While these are wise measures, the bottom line is that the eternal God, who spoke the universe into existence by His power, is and must be our protector. There is plenty in life that we just can't control. In the Bible, Colossians 1:17 says that 'He [Jesus] existed before anything else, and he holds all creation together'. Let's pray for safety for our loved ones and for ourselves. We need the Lord's protection constantly.

'Keep me safe, O God, for I have come to you for refuge,' prays David. We don't know whether he wrote this psalm at a time when his life was in imminent danger, or if he was reflecting on the general course of his life. But the fact is that we all need a place of refuge and protection, and in prayer we can call out to God for help in all situations.

Take some time today to ask God to continue to provide safety and protection for you and your family. Thank Him that your eternal safety is sorted because of Jesus' death and resurrection.

25

26 Wealth

'but their fame will not last. They will die, just like animals.' **Psalm 49:12**

Money, money, money. Got the Abba song in your head now? You're welcome!

In fact, give that song a listen. Even though it's a golden oldie now, the lyrics say a lot about modern society and many people's priorities. The words speak about working all hours just to make ends meet, and how meeting a rich partner or winning the lottery will solve all of life's problems.

Sadly, that's how many people live their lives today – craving more money, thinking that just a little more will make them happy and complete. But a 'little bit more' always seems to require more than the amount we can ever acquire. And we just need to read a few stories of lottery winners whose lives have been devastated after winning a fortune to realise that money is far from being the answer to all of life's problems.

Psalm 49:8 is clear that no amount of money can buy our salvation: 'Redemption does not come so easily, for no one can ever pay enough'. This means that redemption – or salvation, being saved and put right by Christ's sacrifice – was so costly that it could only be earned through Jesus' death on the cross. It's also a reminder that we can't take our wealth with us when we die.

When you pray, you can share with God everything that is going on in your life. This includes money – whether you have a little or a lot. Ask God to help you keep your heart right in relation to money. This ensures that God is number one in your life, even when it comes to money. Our money and our generosity can have the most incredible impact on people's lives. As we pray and seek God, we can receive His guidance even in this area of our lives.

Thank God for His provision in your life. Ask Him to show you areas where you have put your hope in money more than you put your hope in Jesus. Ask Him to show you how to use your money for the good of His kingdom.

26

27 Worship

> 'Give thanks to the LORD, for he is good! *His faithful love endures forever.*' **Psalm 136:1**

I love the emotion that music can create, especially worship music. When I listen to the words of songs I really feel my heart stirring and my mood lightening. Stuff can change just by listening to some God-centred music.

Of course, worship is so much more than just music and singing. Everything we do – from everyday stuff like putting the bins out, to the good stuff like getting out on the bike – can be an act of worship when we do it for God's glory.

I find that when I approach everything in life with an attitude that I am doing it for God, my perspective changes. Joy can be found in even the most mundane tasks when it's offered as an act of worship to God.

It doesn't matter if you're washing the car, stripping paint off a radiator, serving in the military, managing an office or mucking out your daughter's rabbit hutch – any aspect of life can become an act of worship if you do it enthusiastically for God. It says in

1 Corinthians 10:31: 'So whether you eat or drink, or whatever you do, do it all for the glory of God.'

This perspective can impact both how we pray and what we pray for. Even prayer is worshipping God as you pray for others, situations and the stuff in your own life. In the Bible, David had this nailed. He was a man who was able to pray in ways that reflected worship, just telling God everything: the good, the bad and the journey.

The worshipfulness of Psalm 136 is rooted in appreciation of God's goodness. Whatever tasks you go about this week, adopt a mentality of thankfulness. Give thanks to the Lord, for He is good!

---

28 Faith

'Let all that I am praise the LORD; with my whole heart, I will praise his holy name.' **Psalm 103:1**

This psalm is a prayer written by David in which he talks to his own soul, telling himself to 'never forget the good things he [God] does for me'.

I wonder how many of us could give God one minute of praise for all the good things we get from knowing Him? Often we can be great at telling God what we need from Him, rather than praising Him for the many benefits we already enjoy when we place our faith in Him.

This actually is more difficult than it appears. Most of us are better at blaming and criticising than we are at praising. Sometimes we need a good dose of Psalm 103 to rid ourselves of that complaining spirit and replace it with a heart of gratitude to God. David wants to praise God with his 'whole heart' – and that might mean worshipping God even when we really don't feel like it. Let's not do this by halves!

Remember the verses: 'with my whole heart I will praise his holy name' and 'may I never forget the good things he does for me'. This psalm reminds us of five benefits of faith in God that we can use to pray and thank God for, which in turn will really build our faith. The five benefits are forgiveness, healing, deliverance from danger, God's unchanging love toward us and a satisfaction that's deeper than anything the world can offer.

Wow! Each one of these is life-changing, and all five together could change not only *our* lives and *our* world, but the lives of all those around us, and the *whole* world.

Think of all the good stuff that comes with knowing Jesus! Then ask God to show you areas of your life where you might be critical, cynical or blameful. Ask Him to give you a heart of thankfulness instead.

---

29 Creation

'The sea belongs to him, for he made it. His hands formed the dry land, too.' **Psalm 95:5**

I have always been a huge lover of nature and I am fascinated with wild animals, especially marine life. However, the things that I marvel at the most are landscapes. Wherever I go I am drawn to the highest point, just so I can look out over the surrounding areas. Whenever I sit and admire the rolling landscapes around me, I can't help but marvel at the creator who made it all.

One particularly amazing experience for me happened on a trip to Peru. The group was a mix of people who believed in Jesus and those who didn't. On one of our days 'off', we were taken up Mount Huascaran, part of the Andes mountain range, the summit of Huascaran being the highest point in Peru. We were there to visit Pallarcocha glacier lake, some 15,000 feet above sea level. The views were simply breathtaking. It was unlike anything I had ever seen before.

One of the guys in the group who wasn't a Christian came out on a boat trip with me, and together we marvelled at the beauty all around us.

The conversation inevitably led to the idea of there being a creator God, and having been so taken aback by the beauty of the surroundings, this guy had no problems in believing that God was real. By the end of the trip he had accepted Jesus as his Lord and Saviour, all because of the wonder of creation.

A guy in the Bible called Paul wrote this amazing verse in Romans 1:20: 'For ever since the world was created, people have seen the earth and sky. Through everything God made, they can clearly see his invisible qualities—his eternal power and divine nature, so they have no excuse for not knowing God.'

Tell God in prayer what you love about His creation - mountains, valleys, the sea or even your kids. We can thank God for the natural wonders of creation all around us - it's one of the things God has put in place for exactly that purpose!

Take some time today to praise God for the wonder and beauty of His creation. Ask Him to show you ways in which you can help with caring for and maintaining His world.

30 Training for war

'Praise the LORD, who is my Rock.
He trains my hands for war and
gives my fingers skill for battle.'
Psalm 144:1

David was called to be a man of war, and we can
read about his many battles and victories in the
Bible. He doesn't attribute his success in battle to
being a good general or to his own valour, but to
God, who taught and sustained him for the battle.
A lot of the psalms are about David remembering
these punch-ups, and turning them into prayers of
thanks to God for sustaining him.

Today, the majority of us won't be called to
fight the same kind of battles that David fought.
Instead we are warned that our battles are of
the spirit (you might hear this being described
as 'spiritual warfare'). Paul warns us about this
in Ephesians 6:12 where he says: 'For we are not
fighting against flesh-and-blood enemies, but
against evil rulers and authorities of the unseen
world, against mighty powers in this dark world,
and against evil spirits in the heavenly places.'

Each and every day we are tempted by
our desires, lusts and impulses. Our enemy is

deceitful – he will put doubts in our minds, and make us think that it is OK and no harm will come from it. Without Jesus in our lives, we only have our own willpower to fight against all these temptations, and it will simply never be enough. But as Christians, we have the Holy Spirit and a new ability to resist temptation – as new men, the power of darkness is broken.

The Bible doesn't say you won't have sinful desires after you become a Christian, but it does say that the Holy Spirit will help you choose not to satisfy them. It's a spiritual war, but like He did for David, God will provide for and sustain us through the battles. These moments of battle are prayer fuel.

Take some time today to thank God for His protection, strength and wisdom to help you fight the spiritual battles you're up against. Ask Him to show you areas where the enemy has a foothold and how you can overcome them.

30

A note from Nathan

Stephen and I really hope this book on prayer has been helpful. Being able to converse with the living God is one of the most amazing truths and privileges in this life.

If you don't yet count yourself as a follower of Jesus but after reading this book have decided that you want in, then this is the most important prayer of all...

Jesus, thank You that You are the Son of God.

Your battle cry from the cross is my line in the sand. When You called out, 'It is finished,' I know that the power of sin was defeated and now I can be the man I know I need to be.

I'm sorry for trying to fix this without You. I am sorry for my sin. I will turn from it and commit to seeking You and living for You.

I believe in You, Your life, Your death on the cross, and Your resurrection.

Jesus, help me to pray and to seek You. Build my faith stronger and stronger each day.

Be great in me, Jesus. Be a fire that can't be extinguished; be a force that cannot be tamed.

Bring me to prayer. Help me to lift my head in the morning and seek Your face.

As I rest, Jesus, may You be my closing thought.

Until breath has left my body, and I'm on my way to You, be my King.

For Your kingdom, and for Your glory, Jesus, thank You for being my Saviour and friend.

Amen.

If you just prayed this prayer, get in touch with us at **cvm.org.uk/contact** – we want to cheer you on, pray for you, resource you and stand with you.

There's also some more books in this series to help you get to know God better. Have a look on the following page and choose what to read next!

Continue building your relationship with God

Lay the foundations of Christianity and build your relationship with God. Packed with 30 relevant Bible readings, practical points and prayers, these notes will help you navigate through your life and faith.

These Bible notes explore different themes to encourage and challenge. Written by Carl Beech and two guest contributors, each book contains two months of daily readings and prayers.

 Also available in eBook formats

For current prices and to discover the full range, visit
www.cwr.org.uk/themanual